GW00703041

Ending the Royal Farce

The Case for an Elected Head of State

A discussion paper from
Republic

Edited by Cyril Meadows

Republic
London

2003

Published by **Republic** in August 2003
www.republic.org.uk

✳✳✳✳✳✳✳✳✳✳✳✳✳✳✳✳

Republic would like to record its
thanks to the Webb Memorial Trust
for contributing to the cost of
publishing this discussion paper.

✳✳✳✳✳✳✳✳✳✳✳✳✳✳✳

All rights reserved. No part of this
book may be reprinted or
reproduced or utilised in any form
or by any electronic, mechanical, or
other means, now or hereafter
invented, including photocopying
and recording, or in any information
storage or retrieval system, without
prior permission in writing from the
Editor at: **Republic**, PO Box
34851, London W8 5YA.

ISBN 0-9545504-0-4

Copyright © 2003 by **Republic**

Typeset and printed for **Republic** by Quinta Business Services, Meadow View,
Weston Rhyn, Oswestry, Shropshire, SY10 7RN
Tel: 01691 778659 Fax: 01691 777638
Website: www.quintapress.com. E-mail: repinfo@quintapress.com

Ending the Royal Farce

The Case for an Elected Head of State

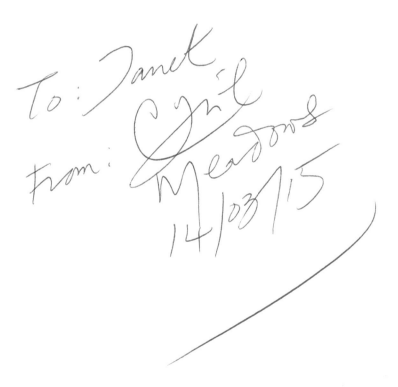

To: Janet,
From: Cyril Meadows
14/03/15

CONTENTS

INTRODUCTION

Republic believes that our system of monarchy is bad for Britain – both in the way it devalues our democracy and in the way it corrodes our society. The only effective solution is to give the British people the right to choose their Head of State under a system of popular sovereignty and to transfer Crown Prerogative Powers to Parliament. While some may argue that the answer to the present royal malaise is the modernisation of the institution of monarchy, it is clear that all the tinkering in the world will not remove its undemocratic nature, nor its archaic and demeaning value-system.

Democracy in this country is no longer a beacon for the whole world, as once we liked to believe. Indeed, by having our sovereignty defined as the 'Crown-in-Parliament', we are tied into a system which is inherently undemocratic, with an unelected Head of State and House of Lords, outdated customs, arcane procedures, and bizarre Ruritanian rituals. Moreover, the executive is able to use a whole range of Crown Prerogative Powers for which there is no democratic accountability – even if a prime minister is by inclination a republican, the availability of these powers makes a monarchist out of him or her.

In short, the monarchical system devalues and enfeebles our democracy.

Recent developments have shown how few are the checks and balances constraining the power of a British prime minister, especially one buttressed by a large Parliamentary majority. We have seen the effective replacement of senior ministers in the decision-making process by unelected advisers, the marginalisation of the Cabinet, and the House of Commons used as little more than a rubber stamp. The claim that a British prime minister has more power than a U.S. president is no exaggeration.

We have heard much recently about creating a 'fairer Britain'. Yet, whenever politicians outline the sun-lit uplands of the new society they hope to create – worlds of 'opportunity for all', 'inclusiveness', and 'merit' – they studiously ignore the existence of the royal family. At the very apex of our society there is an extended group of unelected people, our supposed social 'betters', who inhabit a world of massive exclusiveness, unmerited opportunity, state-funded privilege, and zero accountability. It is our contention that their role diminishes and corrodes our society. We believe that a fairer, more adult and even a more economically dynamic society results when people are given the democratic right to choose their Head of State.

We British are notoriously ignorant of our constitution, which is hardly surprising in view of its 'unwritten' nature. Nowhere is this ignorance more apparent than in the case of the monarchy. Therefore our case against the institution of monarchy is set out in this paper in some considerable detail.

The thrust of this paper is not merely anti-monarchist, however: more important, it is positively pro-republican. For too long the monarchy has survived on a *faute de mieux* basis: many are dissatisfied with it, yet no one has articulated what a republican alternative would be like, what its merits would be, and how it might be achieved. It is hardly surprising that when opinion pollsters ask people 'Do you favour having an elected Head of State?', the majority currently say 'NO', because they have no clear idea of what it would entail. A key purpose of this document therefore is to enable people to clarify their thinking on this critical issue.

We in **Republic** are sometimes accused of being too 'rationalist' in our critique of the monarchy. Don't we realise, we are asked, that many people enjoy the ritual surrounding the monarchy? Don't we understand that such things as emotion and sentiment play as large a part in people's lives as intellect and reason? Our response is emphatically 'YES': we believe that even in a republic there would be a role for state ritual – but it would relate to a modern, transparent, democratic constitutional settlement, not one glorying in its obscurity and unintelligibility.

Clearly, it is all too easy for elected politicians with republican sympathies to be deterred from articulating their views, either because they imagine overt republicanism is a vote-loser, or because it runs counter to their party leadership, or because it is not a big issue in terms of their mail-bags or surgeries. We live in the real world and understand these considerations. Nevertheless, we in **Republic** believe that this matter is becoming potentially urgent. It is time for all like-minded MPs to make their opinions known and give leadership to the country on this issue.

Finally, if having read this document, you come to the conclusion that you share our views, please consider joining us as a member.

August 2003

I

WHY Republic OPPOSES THE MONARCHY

Republic believes that Britain will never become a modern democracy, nor will it be possible to create a fairer and more inclusive society, as long as we languish under the burden of an unelected monarchy. The basis of our opposition to the monarchy falls under three headings:–

1. MONARCHY DENIES US A BASIC RIGHT

It should be a *fundamental right* of the people of this country to elect their Head of State rather than allowing the office to be the sole prerogative of one family and to be held for life. The denial of this right debases our democracy. Indeed, the hereditary principle of monarchy treats the British people as though we were merely chattels, like a flock of sheep, to be passed from one monarch to the next.

We now find ourselves in the anomalous position of being *citizens* of Europe, yet still only *subjects* in our own country. This in a society that claims it prioritises greater equality of opportunity and inclusiveness.

In fact, the concept of monarchy, with its exaltation of the incumbent and their extended family, is a massive confidence trick perpetrated upon our society. Whereas, historically, monarchy was imposed by military force, it now supposedly rests on our voluntary consent. A consent that is so voluntary that it is supported by the Treason Felony Act 1848 which imposes a penalty of life imprisonment on anyone who even 'imagines' the possibility of a republic.

The British people have never been asked whether they wished to elect their Head of State. It is time we were given the opportunity to do so.

2. MONARCHY DEVALUES OUR SYSTEM OF GOVERNMENT

We still retain a political culture centred around *'Her Majesty's Government'* – not *ours* but *hers* – a powerful symbol of the ethos of our whole system. The concept of royal ownership pervades this culture and reinforces the idea that the system does not belong to us.

For it must be remembered that instead of our sovereignty being vested in the people ('We, the people'), it is defined as the *'Crown-in-Parliament'*, yet again distancing us from any real sense of ownership.

On no occasion has *the royal 'ownership' of Parliament* been so amply demonstrated as on *3 April 2002* when both Houses were recalled from their Easter recess to hear MPs and Peers recite tributes to the Queen Mother – tributes which most of them had previously made both publicly and privately. The opportunity to use this occasion for a debate on a major escalation of the Palestinian/Israeli conflict had been denied in advance, but it is to the great credit of some MPs that they refused to be silenced.

To underline the disproportionate role played by the monarch in our political life, it was reported at this time that, because there was a period of 'court mourning' under way, the Prime Minister had to obtain permission from the unelected Head of State to leave the UK for talks with the US President on the critical international situation.

The concept of the monarch owning the government is matched by the doctrine of the monarch being *above the law*. Under the ancient law of *Crown Immunity* government departments or bodies established by statute are protected from prosecution in the criminal courts: such a body breaching health and safety legislation and thereby causing the death of an employee would be immune from prosecution. The monarch is immune from prosecution under employment and race relations legislation. Neither the monarch nor the heir to the Crown is legally *obliged* to pay taxes.

The most recent evidence of the monarch being *above the law* was the collapse of the Burrell case *(November 2002)* from which it emerged that the monarch cannot be required to appear in court as a witness or defendant, and that deference to the assumed wishes of the monarch and the royal family is allowed to inhibit the usual police investigations and court of law procedures.

All MPs are required to swear an *oath of allegiance to the Queen,* irrespective of their personal beliefs. The rules of the House of

Commons (as set out in Erskine May: *Parliamentary Practice,* the Parliamentary 'bible') effectively prohibit MPs from discussing the monarchy in the Chamber.

Our government and Parliament employ a mass of obsolete customs and arcane procedures to endow their activities with a bogus historical provenance and apparent constitutional legitimacy. The prime example is the *State Opening of Parliament* when the elected representatives of the people are summoned to the House of Lords and obliged to pay standing obeisance to the unelected monarch and to the unelected Peers who sit grandly at their ease in the Chamber.

Another example is the *Privy Council* which, as the name suggests, is a rather private affair. It is hardly surprising that few electors are even aware of its existence. Membership of the Council comprises the monarch, senior members of the royal family, the two archbishops, senior figures in the judiciary, and all past and present Cabinet Ministers (who retain their membership – with the title of 'Right Honourable' – for life). The Council meets to proclaim the accession of a new monarch (the 'Accession Council') and to approve the marriage of a reigning monarch. Normal business meetings of the Council take place about once a month: they are chaired by the monarch and require the attendance of a minimum of three Cabinet Ministers, although four are usually present. These meetings deal with formalising acts, under prerogative or statutory powers, which cover mainstream government business concerning e.g. the BBC, universities, the September 2000 fuel crisis, United Nations sanctions. They are held at the convenience of the monarch, usually at Buckingham Palace, or at Balmoral in September. Special meetings are also held to deal with emergencies, to swear in new Cabinet Ministers, and on Maundy Thursday when the 'pricking' of sheriffs takes place – modern government in action.

Britain has one of the most powerful monarchies in the world, but Britons are not widely aware of the *monarch's political power and influence:* the monarch chooses the Prime Minister in the event of a close-run general election, meets the Prime Minister in weekly audiences, and holds Privy Council meetings. The monarch has the right to be consulted by the government of the day and to 'advise and warn' them. The British people may well wonder why the unelected and publicly unaccountable monarch is allowed to interfere in these ways in the governance of the country.

The *Crown Prerogative Powers* are traditional powers of the monarchy from a pre-democratic age which have been devolved by convention to ministers, notably the Prime Minister. Through prime ministerial and governmental use of Crown Prerogative Powers even such matters as making treaties and declaring war are technically exempt from the normal democratic process, and thus the executive is not properly held to account. Not least among these royal prerogative powers are substantial amounts of patronage e.g. the appointment of Peers and the conferring of honours.

Does Britain enjoy open, transparent, accountable government? We think not. The executive and the monarchy enjoy an almost symbiotic relationship, with each realising their mutual self-interest in maintaining the *status quo*.

3. MONARCHY CORRODES AND DIMINISHES OUR SOCIETY

While there has been a tendency in the past to stress the rights-based and democratic arguments against the monarchy, there has been insufficient emphasis on its harmful social and economic effects. This section attempts to redress the balance by identifying the negative areas of impact in some detail.

Although the monarchy, strictly speaking, only covers the incumbent, we actually get an extended family ('The Firm'). They spuriously project themselves as suppliers of a kind of anodyne social cohesion, but the reality is that they leave Britain with an unhealthy social balance sheet.

- **Monarchy is harmfully divisive** – As the champion of social elitism, the monarchy is the embodiment of class, racial, and religious divisions in our society. Although they themselves are state-funded, the royal family act as high-profile patrons of private education which skews opportunity so fundamentally in our society. They are also enthusiastic supporters of private healthcare. Yet, ironically, royals still have NHS hospitals named after them, even though they rarely, if ever, use them. In terms of race, under the present system the Head of State will inevitably come from a white family. In terms of religion, the existing constitutional links between the Head of State and one particular faith are both inappropriate and offensive.

- **Monarchy projects a distorted image of who we are** – Even though Britain seeks to become a more egalitarian and meritocratic society, we have at our social summit an unelected royal family whose very existence is predicated on outdated principles of innate social superiority and unearned privilege. At home, the royal family have become socially dysfunctional. Abroad, they project an outdated and distorted image of what modern Britain is about.

- **Monarchy is socially offensive** – When millions of hard-working families and struggling pensioners in this country live in a state of permanent financial hardship, to see state-funded luxury and extravagance flaunted on high as though they were civic virtues is an affront to any sense of equity in our society.

- **Monarchy demands deference** – In the 21st century, to be expected to show deference to another person purely because of their social status offends the self-worth of every mature adult. Having an extended royal family treated in this way is not some harmless social lubricant. Rather, it encourages a sense of personal inferiority in people. Titles involving 'Majesty' and 'Highness' can only imply 'Lowness' in the rest of us. The deference required by this system serves to erode the self-esteem of certain sections of our society and to foster a climate of cynicism in others. Even the Prime Ministers of Australia, Canada and New Zealand are considered by the Queen to be lower in the pecking order than minor members of the royal family, witness the 'protocol' for the Queen Mother's funeral.

- **Monarchy makes us prisoners of the past** – As an institution based on an outdated ethos, monarchy is inherently backward-looking. Its constant association with military pageantry is a hangover from its imperial past. While much is made of the Commonwealth, we have an honours system largely based on a defunct British Empire. In order to prosper in the modern world, Britain must embrace the present and not be a prisoner of the past.

- **Monarchy devalues intellect** – In Britain the dullest prince is the social superior of a Nobel laureate. Degree-less royals, chosen for their social status rather than individual merit, are appointed as the chancellors of major universities. The implication that high intellectual ability is an automatic by-product of high social status hardly encourages young people from less privileged backgrounds to enter higher education. This message is re-inforced by the toadying respect shown to royal utterances, however banal and ill-informed.

(The Prince of Wales never appears on radio or TV, e.g. on the BBC *Today* and *Newsnight* programmes, to debate and defend his views on controversial issues: why should the media or the public at large accept his opinions uncritically merely because of his birth? Furthermore, if he wishes to make public pronouncements on such matters what has happened to the much-vaunted neutrality and non-intervention of the royal family in affairs of state?)

- **Monarchy trivialises the military** – Members of the royal family appear eager to wear military uniforms, even when civilian dress is more appropriate. What is more, they effortlessly assume top military ranks, bedecking themselves with glittering medals and decorations – often awarded by a close relative. They regularly inspect troops for their personal smartness, yet they do not dress themselves unaided. This military pantomime insults the dedication and professionalism of our armed forces and those who have made genuine sacrifices for our country.

- **Monarchy turns patriotism into a system of personal homage** – In Britain, patriotism (which means love for one's country) gets transmuted into a system of personal homage to the monarch. This is reflected in our national anthem, which has nothing to do with the nation and everything to do with the monarch, and in the extensive system of oaths of allegiance to the monarch required of MPs, members of the armed forces, the judiciary, etc. It should be noted that republicans are patriots even though they are not monarchists.

- **Monarchy demeans our civic culture** – Instead of fostering a sense of equality of worth amongst people, typical royal engagements are characterised by strict rules of social stratification and subservience. In an atmosphere of civic grovelling and petty snobbery, generations of flag-waving children are conditioned to acknowledge their alleged superiors and to accept their status as 'subjects'.

- **Monarchy debilitates civil society** – The system of royal patronage, affecting so many leading voluntary organisations (covering such diverse areas as sport, science, trade, youth, the professions), debilitates our civil society. Such organisations are by convention prevented from having people of genuine personal achievement appointed as their patrons or similar – and are encumbered with the attendant sycophancy of royal involvement. The much-vaunted royal links with charities are allowed to overshadow the genuine efforts of others actually engaged at the 'sharp end' of charitable work. In fact, by meeting such people, it is the royal family who meet their 'betters' every day of the week.

- **Monarchy is the enemy of aspiration** – Although we are now in the third millennium, every non-royal child growing up in Britain knows that, irrespective of their individual merit, they will never be 'good enough' to become Head of State. The system of social hierarchy deriving from monarchy inhibits social mobility and thereby restricts economic opportunity.

- **Monarchy makes us a less open society** – Because we do not enjoy the concept of popular sovereignty, there is an unnecessary distance in the relationship between the people and Parliament. It helps make the latter an exclusive club for the political classes. Having the concept of the Crown attached to the work of government departments also acts as a psychological barrier in terms of people openly questioning officialdom.

- **Monarchy is harmful to the monarchs and their heirs** – In denying the right of ordinary citizens to represent their country as Head of State the hereditary system condemns each heir to the throne to an abnormal (albeit highly privileged and cosseted) upbringing and a pre-ordained future. Whereas the attendant stresses were formerly easy to disguise, modern communications have harshly exposed them. It is also quite unreasonable to expect the monarch to remain as Head of State until death. The present Queen, for example, should already be enjoying the fruits of retirement.

- **Monarchy is costly** – Details of the royal family's income, their financial assets, their land holdings, and their other properties are cloaked in obfuscation and secretiveness, with the 'Palace' camouflaging the facts of the Queen's fortune and deviously creating confusion between her 'personal' assets and those she holds as 'sovereign'. Pending full disclosure and clarification, there is evidence to show that the royal family have in their possession or under their control land, properties, capital, investments, art collections, antiques, jewellery, stamp collections, horses and stud farms, etc. estimated to be worth £20 billion or even more. They are probably the greatest and wealthiest landowners in the country (e.g. in 2000 the Queen drew an income of £7.3 million a year from the Duchy of Lancaster, and the Prince of Wales enjoyed an income of £7.5 million from the Duchy of Cornwall – recently reported to be £9.9 million in 2002).

Yet despite this massive wealth, taxpayers currently provide £63 million (including the Civil List of £7.9 million) each year to support the royal family, and this is only the tip of the iceberg in terms of the total cost to the nation. But even if the services which the royal family claim to provide were given free of charge, they would not compensate for the insidious damage that monarchy inflicts on our society.

(The royal family have a two-faced attitude towards their enormous fortune. On the one hand the Windsors maintain that they need to be 'really wealthy' so as to enjoy financial independence from the government and the state they claim to serve. On the other hand the 'Palace' responds to all attempts to investigate and quantify the Windsors' wealth with statements designed to minimise the extent of their assets and to suggest that they are not at all wealthy in relative terms.)

• **Monarchy debases the concept of duty** – Much is made of the royal family's devotion to duty, yet it is clear that the royals are even more devoted to privilege, precedence of rank, extravagance, and deference from others. For the rest of the nation's citizens, doing one's duty often means considerable self-sacrifice, is normally an instinctive reflex, and does not involve seeking any reward, trade-off or public recognition. The royal family's conspicuous consumption and pampered life-style are well documented, their self-sacrifice in the line of duty is rather less in evidence (e.g. the Queen Mother, Prince Charles, the Duchess of York).

2

WHY WE NEED TO PLAN FOR CHANGE NOW

The institution of monarchy denies the British people a fundamental democratic right, it prevents us from having an open and fully accountable democracy, and it perpetuates a set of outdated and dysfunctional social values that damage our society. Therefore, **Republic** believes, as a matter of principle, that Britain must replace the monarchy with an elected Head of State.

While the target of our campaign is the monarchy itself, rather than the individuals involved, it is self-evident that the circumstances of the present monarch have real relevance when the country is planning for change. Indeed, the stark facts of the matter are that Britain is steadily moving towards a constitutional crisis. The reasons are becoming increasingly apparent.

The Queen was 77 in April 2003. Thus, at some point within the next several years, the question of her succession will arise, either because of her death or abdication, or *de facto* by her delegating her duties increasingly to another member (or other members) of the royal family owing to age or infirmity.

The delegation of duties is totally unacceptable: a modern Head of State must be capable of fulfilling all the duties of their office, or they should be replaced – but *democratically*.

The special personal, marital and family circumstances surrounding those in line of succession under our monarchical system, together with the implications of the Act of Settlement 1701, the Royal Marriages Act 1772, and the monarch's position as the Supreme Governor of the Church of England, are complicating factors likely to trigger a constitutional crisis even before the Queen's term of office comes to an end.

Accordingly, we in **Republic** believe that the enabling mechanism to give the British people a real democratic role in the choice of the next Head of State should be put in place as soon as possible, and not left until events have intervened and forced hurried decisions in an atmosphere of doubt and controversy.

3
WHAT NEEDS TO BE DONE

KEY OBJECTIVE

The replacement of the monarchy by a republic can only be achieved by the democratic choice of the British people. **Republic** will therefore campaign for a referendum on the future of the monarchy, to be held as soon as conditions permit. The question that would be put to the electorate would be as follows:

Do you wish to elect your next Head of State?

In the event of the British people voting for an elected Head of State, then a simple bill would be passed by both Houses of Parliament to abolish the monarchy. The Royal Assent to such a bill would be the last official act of the incumbent monarch. The royal family have always indicated that they will 'go quietly' when it is clear that they no longer enjoy the support of the British people.

A joint committee of both Houses of Parliament would then be established to formulate a longer bill setting out the detailed framework of the new republic. It would build on the work already undertaken in this area by the proposed Constitutional Convention *(see page 21)*. In the interim period, the Speaker of the House of Commons would fulfil the formal duties as Head of State.

INTERIM INITIATIVES

An important precedent was set by Lord Dormand when he raised the question of a referendum on the abolition of the monarchy in the House of Lords on *21 November 2001*. The calling of such a referendum would need the approval of both Houses of Parliament and, as things currently stand, we do not believe that this would be forthcoming in the immediate future. However, the trajectory of politics is impossible to predict.

A major problem that we face is that for far too long in this country there has been a complete lack of openness in discussing the monarchy and the benefits of its replacement by a modern, democratic republic. This has been particularly so in Parliament. It is vital that we seek to change this climate and we aim to take the following initiatives:–

- **Republic** will disseminate the arguments for a republican alternative (as exemplified in this paper) to reduce public ignorance of the arguments involved, and will act as a forum for debate and discussion.

- **Republic** will lobby MPs for the present *oath of allegiance* to the Queen to be abolished and for its replacement by a requirement that MPs should swear to uphold the law and represent their constituents to the best of their abilities. Efforts have already been made in the House of Commons to secure changes to the present procedure – see the Bills introduced by Kevin McNamara MP on *14 November 2000* and on *19 December 2001*.

- **Republic** will support legal action taken by *The Guardian* and others to question the constitutional basis of our monarchy, and to challenge the offensive and blatantly undemocratic legislation still on the statute book that criminalises those seeking to abolish the monarchy (the Treason Felony Act 1848) and discriminates against Roman Catholics (the Act of Settlement 1701) – see the Treason Felony, Act of Settlement and Parliamentary Oath Bill introduced by Kevin McNamara MP on *19 December 2001*.

- **Republic** will press for the virtual prohibition on discussion of the monarchy in the chamber of the House of Commons to be removed and indeed for the monarchy to be debated openly and vigorously.

- **Republic** will campaign for the appropriate Commons select committees (i.e. Public Accounts, Public Administration) and the National Audit Office to investigate how the monarchy conducts its affairs, to establish precisely and comprehensively what assets the royal family own or control (including palaces, homes, other properties, land rights, trusts, share holdings and other investments, art, jewellery, etc.) and what their income is from *all* sources (both 'private' and 'public'), to ascertain whether they are subject to preferential tax or legal treatment, and to determine the true cost of their activities to the taxpayers. It must become an accepted part of the Westminster mindset that the royal family are public servants and need to be made fully accountable for their actions. They must register their interests like any other public servants.

(The Queen paid no income tax or capital gains tax before the memorandum of understanding with the government in 1993 when she agreed to pay these taxes on a *voluntary* basis; it is unclear at what rate (if any) the Queen and the Prince of Wales now *voluntarily* pay these two taxes or on what proportion of their overall income and total capital assets these taxes are actually levied; the Queen was not required by the 1993 memorandum to pay inheritance tax on anything left to her by the Queen Mother – an estimated saving of £20–£25 million; she will also be allowed to pass her own assets to her successor free of inheritance tax.)

- **Republic** will press for the £12.7 billion royal art collection to be made available for permanent exhibition in art galleries throughout Britain, so that *all* the British people will have the opportunity to appreciate some of the fine works of art in their own areas. This is the world's largest private art collection and includes works by such masters as Leonardo da Vinci, Rembrandt, Van Dyck and Canaletto. At present only a tiny percentage of these unique art treasures is ever seen by the public.

- **Republic** will call for the establishment of a Constitutional Convention to discuss the future of the monarchy and to draw up a blueprint for change. Such a convention would comprise representatives of all interested political parties, trades unions, campaigning groups, churches, etc. This would enable the debate to be taken more widely into the public arena.

- **Republic** will support initiatives to limit prime ministerial exercise of Crown Prerogative Powers by requiring the prior assent of the House of Commons. As an example, see the Crown Prerogatives (Parliamentary Control) Bill presented by Tony Benn MP and dated *3 March 1999*.

- **Republic** will support initiatives to ensure that when studying the compulsory National Curriculum topic of 'citizenship' secondary school students are given the opportunity to evaluate objectively the arguments for a monarch or an elected Head of State and to judge for themselves how real their 'citizenship' really is.

4

AN OUTLINE OF THE PROPOSED REPUBLIC

What would a republic be like? Although we cannot pre-empt any future legislation, here are some indications of what lies behind **Republic's** thinking:–

- **Popular Sovereignty** – Instead of sovereignty being vested in the 'Crown-in-Parliament', it would be vested in the British people on the basis of popular sovereignty ('We, the people'). A new National Anthem would be required to reflect the change in sovereignty.

- **An Elected Head of State** – Instead of having an unelected monarch who is deemed to be the superior of all their 'subjects', we would have a directly elected Head of State – a President.

- **The President** – The President would act as the non-executive representative of the people. The position of Prime Minister, as Head of Government, would remain. While the President would carry out state ceremonial duties, these would not necessarily replicate existing ceremonies in either number or content. For example, the opening of Parliament could be effected by the President in an appropriate ceremony in the House of Commons (not in the second chamber as at present), with the Prime Minister reading out the government's proposed legislative programme.

- **Constitutional Powers** – The President's constitutional powers would be strictly limited to: the opening of Parliament; the formal approval of legislation; choosing the Prime Minister (when the occasion demanded); and dissolving Parliament.

- **Dignity but not Condescension** – In carrying out ceremonial duties, the President would be expected to perform them in a style appropriate to one who is first among equals. The President would receive an appropriate salary and the presidential budget would be subject to review by the Public Accounts Select Committee.

- **The Leader of the Country** – The President would act as the leader of the country. As Head of State, they would be expected to represent all that is best about our values, education and culture – and to act as a distinguished ambassador for Britain abroad.

- **Equality before the Law** – The President would be equal before the law (as any other citizen) and would take an oath at the inauguration ceremony to serve the people, uphold the law and protect the constitution. There would be provision for an impeachment procedure.

- **Fixed-Term Office** – The President's term of office would be fixed at five years, with a maximum of two terms to be served by an individual. The presidential election would be held at a separate time from a general election. The President would not be permitted to serve in office beyond the age of 70, and therefore the upper age for election to office would be 65.

- **Eligibility for Office** – The office of President would be open to any British citizen who is an elector and not currently an MP or a Peer/member of the second chamber. Candidates could be drawn from the world of the arts, law, science, commerce, or indeed any other field of endeavour.

- **Faith, Legislature and Commonwealth** – The Church of England would be disestablished, and consequently the President would have no formal constitutional links with any religious faith. Nor would they be a member of the legislature. They would only become head of the Commonwealth if they were elected to the post.

- **No Extended Families** – The President would be required **not** to involve their extended family in the performance of their duties, and would operate from an appropriate but not palatial residence, with modest staffing.

- **Armed Forces** – The President would be the nominal commander-in-chief of the armed forces, although they would be under the direct control of the government of the day. The President would be prohibited from wearing military uniform and would not hold any honorary rank in the armed forces.

- **No Oaths of Allegiance to the President** – All members of the armed forces, together with all other officials and persons currently required to take an oath of allegiance to the Queen, would henceforth swear an oath (or make an affirmation) to uphold the law. No personal oaths of allegiance would be sworn to the President.

- **Elected Second Chamber** – The present mainly appointed but partly hereditary upper house would be replaced with a fully elected second chamber.

- **Honours System** – The current honours system would be simplified and modified – and based only on merit. The award of bogus aristocratic titles, such as 'Sir', 'Baroness' and 'Lord', would cease.

- **Voluntary Associations** – The President would not participate in the wholesale patronage of voluntary associations as practised currently by the royal family.

- **The Former Royal Family** – Members of the present royal family would become citizens like everyone else. They would not be permitted to use titles such as 'Her Majesty', 'His Royal Highness'. Nor would they be permitted to retain their honorary links with the armed forces. Unencumbered by their former royal duties, they would be free to do whatever they wanted.

- **Royal Assets** – The ownership, control and future status of royal palaces, properties, estates, land rights, art collections, capital, etc. and all other financial assets (whether 'private' or 'public') would be the subject of a legally established Parliamentary Commission. Royal assets deemed to be state assets would revert on trust to the nation.

ENDING THE ROYAL FARCE

5
THE BENEFITS OF A REPUBLIC

- **A Revitalised Democracy** – Converting our democracy from one based on a monarchy to one based on a republic would have major benefits in revitalising our whole political system.

- **More Legitimate Government** – The adoption of the principle of popular sovereignty and the elimination of the concept of the 'Crown-in-Parliament' would give increased legitimacy to the whole process of government, with the executive being genuinely accountable to the Commons.

- **Re-connecting People** – The introduction of an open, transparent, democratic constitutional settlement would re-connect voters to the electoral process and reduce the current disengagement.

- **A New Sense of 'Ownership'** – Parliament would henceforth belong to the people. We would view it as 'our' Parliament, not a remote place that we are only allowed to enter courtesy of the political classes. It would also be 'our' government, not 'Her Majesty's'.

- **A New Feeling of Empowerment** – The opportunity given to the British people to actually choose our Head of State would re-invigorate the political process. It would make our society fairer, more democratic, and more open.

- **A Boost to Aspiration** – The equality of worth enjoyed by each citizen would be a powerful stimulus to aspiration in a country all too often seen as the embodiment of class division.

- **Greater Social Inclusiveness** – Because the office of President would be open to any British citizen, irrespective of their family background, race or religion, this would act as a powerful instrument in fostering inclusiveness in our society.

- **No More Life Sentences** – Having a fixed-term period of office removes the disadvantages of having a Head of State foisted on us for life. After a President has been in office for five years and if they are popular, then they will be re-elected for another term (but only one). If they are not popular, they will be removed by the electorate after only one term.

- **A More Human Set of Values** – The values embodied in the office of President would define a society where openness replaces arrogance and secrecy, where social inclusiveness replaces social hierarchy based on birth, and where mutual respect replaces deference.

- **An End to Church Links** – The severing of the constitutional links between the Head of State and the Church of England would reflect the realities of a multi-faith and increasingly secular Britain.

- **A More Valid Representative** – The new republic, through the democratically elected President, would be able to represent Britain in a more valid way, not only to its own citizens, but also to other countries. The President would be able to articulate Britain's values, aspirations, and concerns in a way that is not possible at present, since the monarch is socially divorced from mainstream society. The age of crowns, robes and ridiculous rituals is **over**.

- **Facing the Challenges of the Future** – The creation of a republic would enable us to confront the challenges of the future in a more confident way. While we should be proud of our history, the present system of monarchy encourages us to live in the past, to the detriment of the present and the future.

- **No More Hereditary Wise Men** – In a republic, *what* was said would take precedence over *who* was saying it. The current respect for royal utterances, however intellectually worthless, suggests that the social status of the speaker somehow validates what is being said. Such attitudes seriously hinder the encouragement of intellectual self-confidence among the people at large, from whatever background.

- **Offices For Those Who Merit Them** – By having degree-less royals as their chancellors a number of our universities imply that there is a link between high social status and intellect. In a republic these institutions might wish to consider whether former royals should remain in office or should be replaced by those of genuine personal merit.

- **No More Bogus Generals** – Only those actually serving in the armed forces would be permitted to wear military uniform. The present offensive sight of bogus generals and admirals, bedecked with medals and other decorations, would disappear. The message is clear – in a republic we all have to earn the right to any distinction.

- **An End to Subservience** – Presidential visits around the country would be expected to generate respect, as befits the elected Head of State, but not the current bouts of subservience, condescension and social snobbery. The appointments of lord-lieutenants would lapse.

- **A Healthier Civil Society** – The present unhealthy infiltration by members of the royal family into numerous voluntary associations would be likely to diminish substantially, in proportion to the reduction in their personal status. Instead, patrons could be chosen on the basis of their personal achievement and suitability.

- **The End of State-funded Plutocracy** – The current extravagant life-styles enjoyed by the numerous members of the royal family, courtesy of the taxpayer, would cease. It is certainly no crime to be wealthy, but to have an unaccountable, unelected, state-funded plutocracy institutionalised at the apex of our society is simply no longer acceptable.

- **A More Adult Society** – The cessation of displays of deference to a group of people of no particular distinction, who are neither elected, accountable, nor representative, would have a beneficial effect in making our society more adult and mature – and in reducing growing irritation and cynicism among the British people.

- **A Breath of Fresh Air** – We would no longer have to suffer an institution that disdains any sort of control over or accountability for its actions, witness the recent refusal to register interests. The demise of 'the Palace' – shorthand for all that is secret, undemocratic, arrogant and over-privileged – will be a boon to public life in this country.

- **New Self-Confidence** – It would become a fundamental principle that every child growing up in republican Britain, from whatever background, would learn from an early age that no one was born 'better' than they were and that, if they wished, they too could aspire to become Head of State themselves. This would have considerable psychological impact on individual and collective self-confidence.

- **The People's Celebration** – Each year the freedom-loving citizens of Britain would celebrate Republic Day – the anniversary of the founding of the British Republic and the re-assertion of the sovereignty of the people. Republic Day would be a bank holiday and would be the occasion for all kinds of enjoyable events and activities.

6

Republic's REPLIES TO THE MONARCHIST ARGUMENTS

Apologists for the monarchy are legion. Below we list the arguments wheeled out with monotonous regularity to defend the monarchy or to divert attention from its shortcomings and the urgent need for its abolition. We give **Republic's** reply to each argument.

ARGUMENT I
It's a bargain!

'The monarchy costs us nothing as the income from the Crown Estate (£147 million in 2000) is much larger than the annual Civil List payment of £7.9 million and the other costs now borne by the taxpayer. It sounds like a real bargain.'

Republic's REPLY

Apart from the fact that historically the Crown Estate originated in the seizure of land by kings such as William the Conqueror and Henry VIII, what these apologists conveniently forget to mention is that the original deal behind the current arrangements (dating back to the reign of George III) was not a simple trade-off of Crown Estate income for an annual Civil List payment. In fact, the deal was that Crown Estate income, plus the burden of funding government expenditure (including the cost of the civil service and the judiciary), was to be exchanged for the Civil List payment. It follows, therefore, that were the original deal to be set aside and were the monarchy once more to be in receipt of the Crown Estate income, it would no longer receive the Civil List payment or other contributions to its costs (£55.1 million in 2000), but it would re-assume responsibility for paying for the civil service and the judiciary (current annual cost £16 billion). It is perhaps for this reason that re-negotiation of the original deal has never appealed to the 'Palace'.

The true direct and indirect annual cost of the monarchy to the taxpayers remains to be established by national audit – as does the full extent of the royal fortune *(see pages 15–16 and 20–21)*.

ARGUMENT 2
It works

'The monarchy may not be ideal, but it works; and Britain is unlikely to produce anything better. If it ain't broke, don't fix it.'

Republic's REPLY

When we state that something 'works', this normally means more than just fulfilling a function. An old car may well be able to go from A to B, but if it does so while polluting the atmosphere, consuming too much fuel, dropping oil on the road, having unsafe brakes, and giving its passengers an uncomfortable ride we cannot say that it 'works' other than in the most limited sense of the word. If something really 'works' we mean that it achieves the desired result and effect. The desired result from a modern Head of State is that *the office* should foster a democratic, inclusive and open society where the people are sovereign and citizens enjoy the concepts of equal worth and equal opportunity. On this basis our monarchy is 'broke' and must go.

Britain is most certainly capable of producing a better system than monarchy *(see pages 23–25)*.

ARGUMENT 3
It's magic!

'It would be very unwise to try to deconstruct the institution of monarchy or the role of the incumbent. Monarchy is an inherently magical and mystical concept that is best left undisturbed. Tinkering with our centuries-old system would bring the end of civilisation as we know it. You tamper with institutions at your peril!'

Republic's REPLY

No system of government should be viewed in this way by an educated public. It is important to establish clearly and unambiguously who has power, how that power is derived, and what accountability is associated with that power.

The ghost of Bagehot is often invoked in support of this argument, but his *English Constitution* (1867) is no more than a clever commentary on mid-Victorian politics and the monarchy; it is in no way an integral part of the British constitution.

Bagehot's arguments on the role of the monarchy are now totally outdated (e.g. '… the immense majority of the Queen's subjects … believe they have a mystic obligation to obey her …'; 'We have come to regard the crown as the head of our morality'; 'The masses of Englishmen are not fit for an elective government …'; 'The monarchy … gives … a vast strength to the entire constitution, by enlisting on its behalf the credulous obedience of enormous masses …'; '… the Crown is … a visible symbol of unity to those still so imperfectly educated as to need a symbol.')

ARGUMENT 4
It's God's will

'The present monarch became Queen by divine right, she was anointed by the Archbishop of Canterbury in 1953, and she is the Supreme Governor of the Church of England. The British people have no right to interfere with God's will.'

Republic's REPLY

Britain is an increasingly secular society. To call on divine authority to legitimise a hereditary Head of State is bizarre in such a society. In any case, there is no evidence that any monarch was ever appointed by God. The lesson of history is that heads of state may hold office only with the consent and agreement of the people of their country, and that the 'divine right of kings' is an archaic irrelevance. In modern countries the only legitimacy enjoyed by heads of state is that bestowed on them by the people through the medium of elections – and the British people have always been denied such elections.

ARGUMENT 5
It's a re-assuringly unifying influence on the nation

'Our constitutional monarchy is an important unifying factor, bridging the religious, social, racial and political differences between British people. Especially in times of great uncertainty like the present, the monarchy is a great source of comforting re-assurance to the nation.'

Republic's REPLY

The monarch stands at the top of a hierarchical and class-ridden social structure riddled with innumerable fine distinctions of rank involving medieval titles (Queen, Prince, Duke, Lord, Viscount, Marquis, etc.) and archaic forms of address (Your Majesty, Your Royal Highness, Your Grace, etc.) in which all Britons are required to bow and scrape in deference to their social 'superiors'. Monarchy is an elitist, hereditary system that sends the wrong signals to the British people: it seems to say that what is important is which family you are born into rather than how far you can get on your own merits. The rules of succession mean that the monarchy institutionalises social, religious and racial discrimination.

While popular belief in the quasi-religious nature of the monarchy has declined dramatically over the last two decades, many Britons no doubt enjoy the royal family as they would enjoy a familiar, long-running soap opera; they may well derive a sense of comfort and re-assurance from following the ups and downs of the well known characters who have been around so long that they have entered into the nation's consciousness like those of *Coronation Street*. But this is scarcely a justification for the principle of a monarchical system of government.

ARGUMENT 6
Better than a superannuated politician!

'We don't want someone like a President Thatcher or a President Hattersley! And just think of President Clinton or President Chirac!'

Republic's REPLY

By sneeringly conjuring up the image of a superannuated politician as President of Britain, many monarchists fondly imagine they have found the 'killer riposte' to republicans; and the American and French references are designed to be similarly disdainful and misleading. First, this argument implies that there is something inherently bad about presidents as heads of state by contrast with the inherent virtues and merits of kings and queens – conveniently overlooking Edward VIII and many of his predecessors. Second, and more important, the US and French presidents are also *executive* heads of government (the French President sharing power with the

Prime Minister), whereas we in **Republic** envisage a president as Head of State who would have no executive powers.

In a republic the British people would be able to elect their Head of State e.g. a distinguished lawyer, a leading academic, or a world-recognised medical expert – the choice would be theirs. Even if they elected a superannuated politician, a pop star, or a media celebrity, he or she would nonetheless be the democratic choice of the people. Any Head of State who proved to be unsatisfactory could easily be removed at the next election – something that is absolutely impossible under monarchy. We in **Republic** believe that the British people can be trusted to act maturely and responsibly in electing an appropriate Head of State – as happens in other advanced countries.

ARGUMENT 7
It's a great tourist attraction

'Our tourist industry is massively boosted by the presence of the royal family, with its colour, tradition, pageantry and palaces.'

Republic's REPLY

There is no evidence that monarchy makes any significant contribution to tourism. France has been a republic for over 130 years: the French Republic now attracts three times as many foreign tourists as Britain, and the Palace of Versailles far outstrips Windsor Castle and Buckingham Palace combined as the biggest tourist attraction in Europe. Surveys show that the overwhelming majority of overseas visitors would visit Britain whether there was a royal family or not. The British tourist industry's experience of the year 2001 suggests that factors other than the monarchy are key in determining overseas visitor numbers e.g. foot and mouth disease, the events of 11 September 2001. Even if the monarchy were in fact a great asset to our tourist industry, that would hardly be a principled argument for its retention on constitutional grounds.

ARGUMENT 8
Remember the wonderful charity work

'The royal family make a tremendous contribution in time and effort by acting as patrons to many charities. They provide an invaluable service to the nation and to the people who sometimes get left out of the statutory welfare services net.'

Republic's REPLY

The concept of the 'welfare monarchy' places great stress on the amount of time that members of the royal family devote to supporting numerous charities and the public benefit that results. Indeed, the superfluity of the royals is frequently justified under the convenient rubric of 'charitable work'. The promoters of this concept appear to imply that the demise of the monarchy would see the virtual end of the voluntary services sector in Britain, the drying up of charitable giving, and the end of altruism. Quite the reverse is the case. Freed from the demands of public office, the Windsors would have even more time to devote to charity work. As for the charities themselves, without the hierarchically-based social pressure arising from a royal family, they would feel free to choose patrons distinguished in their own right. Indeed, there is already evidence that charities would rather not have members of the royal family foisted on them as patrons, preferring to have well respected non-royal personalities instead.

Further, we are surely not seriously expected to believe that British people would cease to support charities that help the neediest and most distressed people in the world or medical charities concerned with cancer or heart disease that have struck down their nearest and dearest merely because they no longer had royal patronage?

Does anyone actually imagine that having a member of the royal family as a charity's patron adds one iota to its overall effectiveness? When people are considering whether to give to a charitable organisation, aren't they more concerned with the work it does than with who its patron is? The level of charitable giving in other countries shows that such giving does not depend on royal patronage, and indeed it would be a sad reflection on people if that were so. Some of our best known and most respected charities, such as Oxfam and the Salvation Army, have no royal patronage and this has caused them no obvious disadvantages. Why should it not be the case for other charities?

A final point. As well as being the gracious patrons of numerous charities, members of the royal family are major beneficiaries of charity themselves – witness the lavish apartments provided virtually rent-free at Kensington Palace. Not for nothing has this been described as 'the country's best Housing Benefit system'.

ARGUMENT 9
It's apolitical

'An elected Head of State would be likely to be a politician or somebody who needs the support of a political party to get elected. Politics, politicians and elections always tend to divide, not unite the people. The monarch is an apolitical Head of State, free from party ties, and far more respected than any politician could be. The monarch never interferes in government.'

Republic's REPLY

In a British republic the *office* of Head of State would be above politics, and this fact would transcend any former political affiliations of the incumbent. The House of Commons has for hundreds of years been supervised and controlled by a Speaker, elected from the MPs, who is required to display no political bias in adjudicating matters in the House, and this has in general proved highly successful.

In recent years we have seen independent candidates succeed in local and parliamentary elections without the support of any political party – even sometimes in the face of stout opposition from a political party. In the case of a national election for the non-political position of Head of State there would be even greater opportunities for independent candidates. It would also not be beyond our capacities to devise electoral rules (e.g. on campaigning expenses, TV appearances) to guarantee access to candidates from any section of British society regardless of their financial means or political support.

The idea that British monarchs do not exercise political influence is fanciful. Examples of monarchs acting politically are: George V's invitation to Ramsay McDonald to form a coalition government in August 1931; George VI's endorsement of Chamberlain's Munich policy in 1938 by inviting him on to the balcony of Buckingham Palace to acknowledge the plaudits of the public; and the present Queen's decision to invite Edward Heath to form a government in February 1974. *(See also page 11)*. Monarchs play a political role, but they are not accountable to the British people.

ARGUMENT 10
It's a stabilising factor

'The sovereign personifies national cohesion, Commonwealth unity, and political stability.'

Republic's REPLY

The claim that the sovereign or monarch personifies national cohesion, Commonwealth unity, and political stability is laughable.

It is difficult to think of a time when the social life of this country was in such turmoil as at present, bearing in mind the massive disparities of wealth, educational opportunity and healthcare provision, soaring rates of violent crime, the race riots in our cities, and the social disintegration caused by steeply rising levels of drug and alcohol abuse.

The unity of the Commonwealth must be open to question when its two most populous member countries – India and Pakistan – have recently been in a state of nuclear stand-off. The situation in Zimbabwe has factionalised opinion among Commonwealth countries. Meanwhile, the British monarch is seen to be quite irrelevant to any resolution of these issues.

Political stability at Westminster is in reality political sclerosis, with our executive-dominated Parliament a pitiful parody of modern, accountable democracy, and with voter abstentions at an all-time high; as for politics in its wider sense, the monarch's contribution to political stability did not apparently extend to the 30-year civil war in Northern Ireland, the 1984 miners' strike, the 1990 Poll Tax riots or the September 2000 fuel crisis – to give just a few examples of instability.

ARGUMENT II
It's a symbol of continuity

'The monarchy provides a powerful symbol of continuity and links with our past. There are no elections for Head of State to break the continuity of office.'

Republic's REPLY

Continuity is provided more by the exceptional long-lived monarchs e.g. Victoria or the present Queen, than by the system of hereditary succession itself. Edward VIII's brief reign in 1936 is notable in this context. Such continuity as we may experience under a long-lived monarch is achieved at a high price since we lose the democratic right to choose our Head of State or to remove an unsatisfactory Head of State. Our system of government is also devalued, and we remain subjected to a corrosive social value system based on deference, privilege, snobbery and exclusiveness.

ARGUMENT 12
It's a glorious part of our history

'Britons value the monarchy as representing their great history. If the House of Windsor ceased to reign over us, it would be the "end of history". The legitimacy of the monarchy has been sanctified by 1000 years of history.'

Republic's REPLY

Rapine, pillage, pestilence, mass starvation, bear-baiting, and public executions have also been part of our history, but over the centuries we have managed to rid ourselves of them all. So should it be with the outmoded institution of monarchy. The monarchy will always be part of our history, but we must now have the self-confidence to make it become well and truly history.

Moreover, to view our history as being predominantly a record of the reigns of sundry kings and queens is to lose all sense of proportion. Most British monarchs have enjoyed the fruits of office simply as a birthright, and few have distinguished themselves by their personal achievements. British history is the history of the British people *in toto* and is more truly represented by those who have achieved greatness by their own merits e.g. Shakespeare, Milton, Wren, Newton, Watt, Telford, Nelson, Austen, Faraday, Darwin, Brunel, Nightingale, Watson-Watt, Churchill, Hodgkin. It is the story of independent thinkers, ingenious inventers, adventurous entrepreneurs, and political and social pioneers far removed in mindset from the stifling conformity and obsessive pre-occupation with protocol, precedence and social rank characteristic of court life in Britain.

A consideration of the origins and evolution of the British – or English – monarchy is instructive. Far from having 'noble' or 'glorious' beginnings, the monarchy was essentially the outcome of armed struggles between the bandit chiefs or warlords of their day, culminating in the seizure of power and land by the bandit victor. The key example of this phenomenon was William the Conqueror – 'landing with ... armed *banditti*, and establishing himself king of England against the consent of the natives' (Thomas Paine).

The English royal family did not, of course, reign uninterruptedly over the United Kingdom for the following 1000 years. The sovereignty of English monarchs was opposed and contested across the British Isles for centuries. A number of monarchs were eliminated in violent circumstances. Wales was not united with England until 1543; the Kingdom of Great Britain (i.e. England and Scotland) was not established until 1707; the Kingdom of Great Britain and Ireland was not created until 1801; and the United Kingdom of Great Britain and Northern Ireland dates only from 1922. The House of Windsor was created as recently as 1917 – when the royal family changed their name from Saxe-Coburg-Gotha to conceal their German origins.

In modern times the royal family have exploited their privileged position to secure massive tax exemptions and pursue a policy of ruthless self-aggrandisement in terms of wealth, land and properties at the expense of an unsuspecting populace. The passage of 1000 years has by no means legitimised or sanctified the original or subsequent usurpations of power and expropriations of land: on the contrary, Britain needs Land Reform and an elected Head of State as never before.

ARGUMENT 13
It's better for ceremonial occasions

'No elected or appointed person could perform the state ceremonial roles as well as the monarch who is born, bred and trained to do this job.'

Republic's REPLY

This argument presupposes that state ceremonies should be carried out only by aristocratic people with distinctive accents, expensive clothes, and a condescendingly patronising manner, and that Britons should feel flattered to play any part – be it ever so humble and deferential – in such events. We believe that we should have an elected Head of State drawn from any sphere of society, regardless of birth, whose conduct reflects the equality of all citizens. An elected President would be expected to carry out his/her duties with all due dignity and entirely without condescension.

ARGUMENT 14
An aristocrat is best for the international scene

'Having a high-born aristocrat as Head of State brings Britain international prestige and status that no elected commoner could possibly provide.'

Republic's REPLY

The 50 years since the Queen ascended the throne have seen the slow but inexorable decline of Britain as a world power and as an economy (relative to other countries). The Queen's longevity may have made her something of a permanent fixture on the international stage, but it is difficult to see how an aristocratic figurehead with the archaic trappings of crowns and jewels adds anything to Britain's prestige or status. A Head of State who demands bowing or curtseying from other heads of state and who never gives an interview or makes a spontaneous public utterance is very odd, nay eccentric: it certainly doesn't make us the envy of the world.

ARGUMENT 15
Abolition of the monarchy isn't a priority

'The government has higher priorities than the abolition of the monarchy i.e. the bread-and-butter issues such as the NHS, education, transport, crime, welfare, and race relations'.

Republic's REPLY

If the argument that the government has higher priorities had been accepted throughout Britain's history we would have had no constitutional progress at all e.g. no Reform Act of 1832, no Votes for Women in 1918 & 1928, no expulsion of hereditary peers from the House of Lords in 1999.

But monarchy is not just a constitutional issue, it is a social and economic issue. Having a democratically elected Head of State would define our society in a different way, creating the conditions for a more egalitarian social climate which would be likely to help us to address the important bread-and-butter issues more effectively.

ARGUMENT 16
Remember the Queen's experience

'The present Queen has served the country for 50 years without putting a foot wrong. She has unrivalled experience of politics and events. She's a priceless asset to the nation.'

Republic's REPLY

The logic of the argument that longevity in office is the key merit of a monarch is that a putative successor, starting with no previous experience of office, would be at a serious disadvantage (or would even be unfit for office).

The qualities and experience of a particular incumbent are irrelevant to a rational consideration of the principle of monarchy. We in **Republic** are concerned about the institution of monarchy and the grave damage it causes: we have no interest in *ad personam* comments about the present incumbent.

Nevertheless, it is priceless institutional effrontery for an unelected Head of State to dictate to Parliament (as in *April 2002*) and thus to the British people how she intends to reign over us and for how long. Are the British people in control of their Head of State or vice versa?

Furthermore, the Queen's intervention through her son in the Burrell case (*Regina v Burrell* at the Old Bailey, *October-November 2002*) calls into question both her judgement and her supra-legal status (*see also page 10*).

ARGUMENT 17
Remember the Duke's and the Prince's youth work

'The Duke of Edinburgh (via his Award Scheme) and the Prince of Wales (via the Prince's Trust) do enormously valuable work in helping young people who would otherwise have slipped through the system.'

Republic's REPLY

We agree that both of these schemes have been generally successful, but it is unlikely that similar schemes would not have emerged if we had had no monarchy over the last 50 years. It will be remembered that the Boy Scout movement was not founded by a member of the royal family. Excellent work of this type does not entitle people to be Head of State, nor is it any kind of justification for hereditary monarchy.

ARGUMENT 18
Reform not abolition

'The monarchy does, of course, need to be reformed and updated, but there is no need to replace it. The royal family have themselves already established a 'Way Ahead' group to investigate how they may make changes.'

Republic's REPLY

The royal family's 'Way Ahead' group has made little progress since it was set up. Any changes it proposes are likely to be extremely limited in constitutional scope and social impact, though worthy in themselves (e.g. the end of primogeniture and royal discrimination against Catholics, giving up the royal train), and would be designed to offer the concessions the royal family judge necessary to secure their survival for the foreseeable future: the classic manoeuvre of monarchies down the centuries.

In fact, the 'Way Ahead' group has no authority from the British people to consider 'modernising the monarchy' and shows little inclination to take instructions from the people: in 2001 a large number of MPs invoked Parliamentary procedures to request the royals to register their financial interests, like all other public servants, but the MPs were rebuffed. The future of the monarchy must, of course, be decided by the British people as represented through Parliament, not by the royal family: let *our* will, not *their* will, be done.

While interim initiatives as laid out on *pages 19–22* should certainly be undertaken, proposals to 'reform' the monarchy, whether they emanate from the 'Way Ahead' group or elsewhere, miss the point. The 'Palace' can slim, trim and spin as much as it likes, but it cannot escape the over-riding issue: that our system of hereditary monarchy denies the British people the fundamental democratic right to choose their Head of State.

ARGUMENT 19
The monarchy will fade away

'There's no need to get excited about abolishing an institution that an increasing number of British people think will no longer exist in 50 years' time. The monarchy will fade away of its own accord in due time.'

Republic's REPLY

This is a disingenuous argument designed to disarm critics of the monarchy and discourage them from campaigning for abolition. As both monarchists and republicans know, if we simply wait for institutions to change of their own accord nothing will happen. Who would have thought that after Lloyd George's attempt to reform the House of Lords in 1911 it would take another 88 years to remove most (but not all) hereditary peers from the upper house? History shows that royal dynasties cling tenaciously to power and the Windsors are unlikely to be any different in this respect. Just waiting around for something to happen has the great disadvantage that nobody takes the trouble to develop a clear idea of what a republican alternative would be like. Meanwhile, the social, political and constitutional dysfunctionality of the monarchical system continues to blight our society.

ARGUMENT 20
It's harmless: we are really a republic!

'Of course, the monarchy is harmless and irrelevant. The powers of our constitutional monarch are severely circumscribed, as everyone knows. To all intents and purposes we already have a British Republic.'

Republic's REPLY

The monarchy is by no means harmless or irrelevant: it casts a pall over the whole of British society and has a direct impact on the running of the country. It denies us our basic right to choose the Head of State, it devalues our system of government, and it diminishes and corrodes our society. It is fundamentally bad for Britain.

Although many people assume that the monarch's powers are negligible, we have shown on *page 11* how extensive is the monarch's political reach.

The cynical assertion that Britain is in effect a republic is calculated to make republicans wonder whether they are not making much ado about nothing. It is sophistry to define 'republic' in such a way as to make it applicable to Britain in 2003. By any normal criteria a republic must have an elected Head of State, popular sovereignty, and general acceptance of the equal worth of all its citizens. Britain currently satisfies none of these criteria.

CONCLUSION

The case for an elected Head of State in Britain has been laid out exhaustively in this paper. But however convincing the case may be in itself, we in **Republic** do not underestimate the powerful forces arrayed against any change to the *status quo*.

Until roughly the last decade of the 20th century the British monarchy was substantially shielded from critical comment in the media and there was precious little opportunity for analytical discussion of our monarchical system of government. British people were conditioned into believing that any critique of the monarchy was somehow subversive and unpatriotic. Republican sympathies were regarded as virtually treasonable. Even in April 2002 academic media pundits felt able to assert that any TV viewer who was not stirred by the ceremonial of the Queen Mother's funeral could hardly be British.

Though freedom of speech on the monarchy has begun to assert itself in the media in recent years, much of the press coverage is concerned with the vicissitudes of life in the royal family and does not involve in-depth analysis of the constitutional, political and social issues raised by Britain's hereditary Head of State and the associated panoply of pomp, privilege and plutocracy. Nor in our supposedly mature democratic society do the media devote much time or space to proposals for an alternative system. Debating the monarchy is still virtually taboo in the House of Commons.

The monarchy has been able to survive partly because of the absence of open debate and discussion, and partly because of a certain capacity to react to change and re-invent itself. It also has powerful allies in the 'pragmatic' politicians: those in control of the government of the day. The latter may well advance some of the arguments listed on *pages 31–44,* with particular emphasis on the government's higher priorities: transport, health, education etc. But they are fundamentally reluctant to relinquish the non-accountable powers they exercise under the secretive and Byzantine conventions, precedents and unwritten rules of our monarchical system, and they do not wish to miss out on the patronage available under the system. They also appreciate the opportunities to exploit royal occasions such as the State Opening of Parliament, funerals, golden weddings, and jubilees: 'modern' government with a feudal face.

We in **Republic** believe that, whether politicians are currently in power or are 'governments-in-waiting', it is now time for them to put the national interest before party-political and power-driven considerations. Surely in their hearts the majority of our politicians favour fully representative democracy with an elected Head of State, proper parliamentary scrutiny of the executive, and complete accountability of public servants? Wouldn't they prefer large-scale participation in elections and public life by well-educated, non-deferential **citizens** who have a sense of 'ownership' about their country and their government? We hope that many politicians will be only too eager to break the Commons taboo on debating the monarchy and help the country to avoid the constitutional crisis we anticipate.

We trust that all those, especially MPs, who read this paper and are convinced by the arguments in favour of an elected Head of State will join with us in campaigning and pressing at every opportunity for the measures and the legislation that will lead to the democratic creation of a British Republic.

APPENDIX

EXTRACTS FROM *HANSARD*

Parliamentary copyright material from *Hansard* is reproduced with the permission of the Controller of Her Majesty's Stationery Office on behalf of Parliament.

These extracts exemplify valiant efforts made to raise the issue of monarchy in Parliament and the difficulty of starting democratic debate, eliciting reasoned responses, or securing unequivocal and complete information in reply to legitimate questions.

Hansard Extract No. 1
House of Lords 21 November 2001
The Monarchy

Lord Dormand of Easington asked Her Majesty's Government:
Whether they will call a referendum on the abolition of the monarchy.

The Lord Chancellor (Lord Irvine of Lairg): No, my Lords.

Lord Dormand of Easington: My Lords, I thank my noble and learned friend for that unambiguous Answer. However, has he taken into consideration that opinion polls in recent years have consistently shown decreasing support for an hereditary monarchy? Does he accept that most people now believe that an elected head of state is more relevant to the 21st century?

Noble Lords: Oh!

Lord Dormand of Easington: My Lords, I am glad of all the support that I am receiving. In view of those and other factors is it not necessary in a democracy such as ours to ascertain the views of the electorate on such a fundamental issue?

The Lord Chancellor: My Lords, the Government believe that the national interest and desire is for the country to remain a constitutional monarchy in its present form. The Sovereign personifies national cohesion, Commonwealth unity and political stability. We believe that support for the monarchy in the United Kingdom is rock solid. In surveys over the past 30 years it has been consistently above 70 per cent, while support for a republic has varied between a mere 15 and 20 per cent. The noble Lord mentioned opinion polls. The Queen's approval rating in opinion polls is a very substantial distance beyond that to which politicians and other groups might reasonably aspire.

Lord Strathclyde: My Lords, the noble and learned Lord's totally unambiguous Answer is widely welcomed throughout the House and by this party in particular. But what does the noble and learned Lord think the general public will make of a senior Back-Bencher and former chairman of the parliamentary Labour Party asking a Question such as this?

The Lord Chancellor: My Lords, the noble Lord is well entitled to ask the Question which he has asked, and the Government's position has been clearly stated by me.

Lord Corbett of Castle Vale: My Lords, as my noble and learned friend is considering the issue of a referendum, will he use whatever influence he may feel he has with the Government to try to persuade them to hold a referendum on the siting of the national football stadium so that football fans and other citizens can be given the opportunity to back the superb bid by Birmingham and Solihull, made on the back of their international airport, their railway station and their motorway network, to place the home of the national sport at the heart of the nation?

Noble Lords: Hear, hear!

The Lord Chancellor: My Lords, I have ruled out a referendum on the subject matter of the Question, but I have noted the support for the noble Lord's observations on the different subject which he addressed.

Lord St John of Fawsley: My Lords, would it not be singularly inappropriate, and, indeed, curmudgeonly, to hold a referendum at the same time as we celebrate the Queen's Golden Jubilee? Would it not be more appropriate for the Government to organise a national vote of thanks to Her Majesty for the way in which over 50 years she has discharged her duties with skill, dedication and diplomacy?

The Lord Chancellor: My Lords, I am sure that the noble Lord speaks for almost everyone in the House. His question gives me the opportunity to say that the timing of the Question is not of the best on the eve of Her Majesty's Golden Jubilee, marking 50 years of dedicated service by the Queen to the nation and the Commonwealth.

Lord Paul: My Lords, the monarchy is such a tremendous asset to this country. Why do we want to confuse the public by a referendum?

The Lord Chancellor: My Lords, my belief is that the public have no interest in a referendum on this subject.

Lord Smith of Clifton: My Lords, will the noble and learned Lord use his professional knowledge to instruct the House whether the presidential style assumed by Mr Tony Blair is lese-majesty?

The Lord Chancellor: My Lords, we have a strong Prime Minister; we do not have a president.

Lord Hughes of Woodside: My Lords, does not the Question of my noble friend Lord Dormand illustrate the vigorous independence of Back-Benchers in your Lordships' House which the Leader of the Opposition claims to espouse?

The Lord Chancellor: My Lords, Members of this House are independent as well as some being affiliated to parties.

Lord Clarke of Hampstead: My Lords, does my noble and learned friend agree that, in conducting its duties and commitments to the voluntary and charitable sector, the Royal Family provides an invaluable service to the nation and to the people who sometimes get left out of the statutory services net?

The Lord Chancellor: My Lords, I can agree with that question wholeheartedly. The Prince of Wales, the Duke of Edinburgh and the Princess Royal are well known as supporters of voluntary causes. I mention, for example, the Save the Children Fund, of which the Princess Royal has been president since 1970, The Duke of Edinburgh's Award scheme, the World Wildlife Fund, Macmillan Cancer Relief and the Outward Bound Trust. Last, and certainly not least, I mention the Prince's Trust, through which the Prince of Wales has made a difference to the lives of tens of thousands of young people, including many of the most disadvantaged.

Lord Stoddart of Swindon: My Lords, is the noble and learned Lord the Lord Chancellor aware that I agree entirely with what he said about the monarchy but that I deplore, and believe it to have been entirely reprehensible, that my noble friend should have been shouted down in the manner that he was in asking a perfectly pertinent and legitimate question?

The Lord Chancellor: My Lords, I have already said that the noble Lord was well entitled to ask the Question that he did.

Hansard Extract No. 2
House of Commons 9 July 2002
Royal Finances

Norman Baker (Lewes): I am grateful for the opportunity to have half an hour to discuss with the Minister royal finances and the Government's attitude toward them.

I recognise that the present arrangements are steeped in antiquity in many ways, and that some aspects have been unchanged for centuries. However, other aspects were adversely changed, from the point of view of the taxpayer, during the 20th century. The key argument that I shall deploy is that the arrangements are unsuitable for the 21st century, and I am keen to persuade the Government of that point of view. I recognise that there have been publications in recent days relating to royal finances. That is a step forward, and if the Government had any say in encouraging that, I congratulate them on taking that line. The basis of my argument is that all citizens in this country should be treated equally on taxation – I include the Queen as a citizen, if I am allowed to do that. Royal finances should be transparent, as one would expect because public money is being spent. I make a distinction between matters that are properly private finances and those that are public finances. There should be proper control and auditing of the way in which public money is spent on royal finances, which is the case for every other area of public expenditure. There is no reason why royal finances should be different.

I shall address equal treatment. It is difficult to justify one individual, who happens to be the Head of State, having absurdly preferential terms of tax payment compared with other people in the country, particularly since the person who holds that office happens to be very rich. How can it be justified that the monarch is exempt legally from income tax, capital gains tax, inheritance tax and requirements to which everybody else in the country must conform? That position seems to be indefensible.

I accept that the 1993 memorandum of understanding under the Conservative Government represented a step forward and attempted to regularise the position. However, the memorandum outlined a situation in which the present Head of State – the principle does not extend into the future, except in so far as it relates to the Prince of Wales, who also agreed to the memorandum – agrees to pay voluntarily income tax and capital gains tax, but not inheritance tax. Of course, the Queen therefore received an estimated windfall of between £20 million and £25 million due to the sad death of her mother. That represents a great loss to the Chancellor, and as he is notoriously prudent in his attempts to control public finances, no doubt he did not welcome that big hole appearing in the Government's income stream.

The memorandum was presented as a step forward in 1993, and recognised matters by putting them on paper. However, George III paid income tax when it was first introduced in 1799 – there was nothing exceptional about that. When income tax returned in 1842 – it was abandoned for a period – Queen Victoria and Edward VII paid it. The requirement of the monarch to pay income tax was removed only during the reign of George V in the past century in exchange for paying the costs of visiting Heads of State. The idea that monarchs are exempt from income tax is not traditional, but a recent idea from the past century.

During George VI's reign in 1937–38, his requirement to pay income tax on his private income was removed. I tried to find out more about that after being directed to it by various august publications, but I understand that the relevant files on the agreement have been destroyed. I wonder if the Minister can confirm that. It would be very unfortunate if those files have been destroyed.

The 20th century has been seen as a time when steps were taken to regularise royal finances by bringing them into line with the taxes and arrangements applicable to everyone else in the country. Actually, however, the arrangements are even more beneficial to the holder of the office of Head of State.

The 1993 memorandum of understanding says that the present occupant of the post will pay income and capital gains tax voluntarily. It is not clear, however, at what level that tax will be paid. It is not mentioned in the memorandum, the justification being that it is improper to discuss individual tax arrangements. I would be happy to accept that argument were normal taxation arrangements to apply to that individual as to all others. However, as the arrangements are unique, we have a right as taxpayers to know what they are.

I should be interested to know what the voluntary arrangements have meant in practice since 1993. Do income tax payments made by the present monarch correspond to those that would be required were she subject to mandatory taxation requirements, as everyone else in the country is? Or, for example, has she sought not to pay the 40 per cent. top rate? That needs clarification, because it is not clear from the memorandum of understanding.

From my understanding of the document, voluntary tax could be a very low taxation yield indeed. It could even voluntarily disappear altogether. There are historical precedents for taxes voluntarily being paid by members of the royal family and those contributions subsequently withering on the vine. Unless the Minister tells me otherwise, we have no guarantee that taxation is paid as it is by a normal citizen, and that that practice will continue.

Equal treatment is a matter of fairness and equity. It is – dare I say – in line with the Government's general philosophy towards the application of taxation. Therefore, I hope that the Minister will be sympathetic to those points. Historically, such arrangements are not ancient, as I have said. Many are the benefits that the Government of the day were persuaded of during the 20th century – Parliament had little say in the matter. Paragraph 31 of the 1993 memorandum of understanding states that arrangements can be changed at the will of the monarch – not the Government. I therefore wish to ask the Minister whether that clause has been invoked since the memorandum was introduced.

I have dealt with the first point – that of equal treatment for citizens. The second point of principle is one of transparency. Again, no doubt largely due to historical accident, there is not the transparency in royal finances that we would wish to see. Certainly, there is not the transparency that would apply in other areas of public finance. For example, the status of the Duchies of Cornwall and Lancaster is unclear. The Duchy of Cornwall is entitled to benefits that are allegedly given away to the monarch, even though the title is traditionally held by someone else. Even if a case could be made for unique taxation benefits for the monarch, it is unclear why they should also be extended to the Duke of Cornwall.

The Duchy of Lancaster is regarded as a private income for the monarch, yet there is confusion about which elements of the privy purse are used for public and private purposes. That is unclear and needs to be made clear. It is also historically unclear why Duchy of

Lancaster lands and assets were not transferred, as the Crown estates were, to Parliament in 1760, and why they subsequently retained that unique status. The status of other assets held

'by the Queen in the right of the Crown',

such as the royal collection, is unclear, too. What is the Minister's understanding of the status of those assets? My understanding is that they are state, or public, assets that are owned by this country's citizens but happen to be held for the country by the monarch of the day. That would seem to be justified by the fact that they are not subject to the taxation treatment expected of private assets. In the unlikely event that this country becomes a republic at some distant point, would assets such as the royal collection pass to the state, or to the deposed monarch? It would help if the Minister would confirm that they are state assets, so that we are clear about the status of the royal collection and other such matters.

We also need a public inventory of assets held in that way, such as the royal collection, that are regarded not as the private property of the Queen or whoever happens to be Head of State at the time but as being held by the Queen or monarch for the public good. We need to make it clear what is public, and a public inventory of such assets would help.

It would also help if the Minister would make clear the position of gifts. My understanding is that gifts provided by the monarch or members of the royal family for visiting Heads of State are paid for out of public funds, although I am not sure whether from the privy purse or the civil list. Is that so? Do gifts received by the monarch in return from visiting Heads of State become public property, or are they regarded as the Queen's private assets? I am sure that the Minister would agree that it would be invidious if the state pays for gifts but the Queen keeps gifts that she receives, and I hope that she will tell me that that is not so.

Transparency requires public scrutiny of the accounts. I recognise that we are moving towards that, but we are not there yet. It requires the National Audit Office and the Public Accounts Committee to be involved, just as they are in the case of other major pockets of Government expenditure. I see no reason why royal finances should not be subject to that rigour. Knowing how keen the Chancellor is to have tight control of public finances – he does well in doing so, in many respects – I cannot believe that he is happy with such a loose arrangement that involves many millions of pounds.

On proper control of public money, it is appropriate to look at the civil list. I notice that £37 million has built up in balances – a huge amount. Indeed, it increased last year, from £35 million, as it is gaining interest and is not being spent or reclaimed by the Government. The reason for that goes back to 1990, when an absurd settlement was reached that allowed an inflationary increase of 7.5 per cent. a year. That was welcomed by the then Prime Minister, Margaret Thatcher, and the then Leader of the Opposition, Neil Kinnock. It was left to some of the Minister's Back-Bench colleagues to question whether a 7.5 per cent. inflation estimate was sensible. They turned out to be right to do so, because it was not, and a huge balance has built up over that period.

We need to be able not simply to freeze the civil list, as that allows balances to increase, but to find a mechanism to reclaim some of the money held there, return it to the Exchequer and use it for decent public purposes. I would welcome the Minister's comments on that.

The civil list should recognise the contribution of the Head of State, his or her spouse and the heir to the throne. It is inappropriate in the 21st century for it to be so exhaustive and to include so many minor royals. That arrangement may have been appropriate 200 years ago, but it is not appropriate today. It also reflects the fact that the present royal family, notwithstanding the spin from the palace that they cost us only 58p a year each – that does not, however, include all the tax breaks – is more expensive than other European monarchies.

This debate has been not about whether we should have a monarchy, but about equal treatment of everybody's finances, transparency and proper control of public money – matters that the Government hold dear. To those who think that the debate is about the monarchy, it could be argued that the changes that I advocate would do more to solidify the foundations of the royal family and the monarchy than do the present arrangements, which leave them open to justifiable criticism on financial grounds.

The Paymaster General (Dawn Primarolo): I thank the hon. Member for Lewes (Norman Baker) for the clarity with which he advanced his arguments and sought information about the royal finances. I spoke to him briefly before the debate and will endeavour to answer his every question. However, if, in scrutinising the record afterwards, he finds that I have missed anything or run out of time, I will certainly write to him.

The hon. Gentleman talked about unique arrangements, the importance of transparency, and the auditing arrangements. He then asked specific questions about those arrangements. He asked why Her Majesty the Queen's circumstances have changed with regard to the agreement's being voluntary, whereas her predecessors may have paid. However, such payments have always been purely voluntary and, over the years, as the burden of taxation increased and the monarchy's financial position changed, successive sovereigns have had to take a view on how far that voluntary agreement went.

The hon. Gentleman has considered the memorandum of understanding carefully, which details the voluntary arrangements on income tax, capital gains tax and inheritance tax for the Queen and His Royal Highness the Prince of Wales. I draw the hon. Gentleman's attention to that issue in particular, because, as he rightly said, the debate is not about whether we should have a constitutional monarchy, but about public finances. It is important to draw clear lines between private monies in the tax system and those assets that are held by the sovereign on behalf of the nation. However, paragraph 9, under the inheritance arrangement, states towards the end that the monarchy as an institution needs sufficient private resources to enable it to continue to perform its traditional role in national life and to have a degree of financial independence from the Government of the day. That principle must be balanced with the principles on which the hon. Gentleman concentrated: transparency and paying tax in the circumstances in which other citizens do.

The basis for the memorandum of understanding is the long-standing rule of statutory construction that statutes do not bind the Crown, including the Queen in her private capacity, unless they are expressly enabled to do so by necessary implications, and legal advice has confirmed that. The arrangements in the memorandum were discussed and agreed between the Government and Her Majesty. At the time the Government said that they welcomed the Queen's and the Prince of Wales's offer to pay tax voluntarily, and that the arrangements in the memorandum were a fair and proportionate way in which to take that into account. In law, the sovereign is not liable to pay unless required explicitly to do so by an Act of Parliament. Given that the sovereign is entitled to the revenues when there is no

Duke of Cornwall, Crown exemption applies also to income received by the Prince of Wales from the Duchy of Cornwall.

Since 1993, Her Majesty the Queen and His Royal Highness the Prince of Wales have paid tax on voluntary arrangements agreed with the Government. That means that most sources of income, such as private investment income money, profit and losses from farming at, say, Sandringham, Balmoral and Windsor, or from opening to the public the houses and gardens at Sandringham and Balmoral, are dealt with in accordance with the usual tax rules. However, the memorandum of understanding includes special arrangements. The hon. Gentleman asked whether income tax is paid at the usual level, and the answer is yes. Capital gains is another example. It is not a negotiable lower rate.

Income tax is paid on all private sources of income. The memorandum of understanding includes provision for calculating the private taxable proportion of the Prince of Wales' income from the Duchy of Cornwall. Tax is also paid on the Queen's privy purse income, which includes income received from the Duchy of Lancaster to the extent that it is used for personal purposes. The hon. Gentleman asked a specific point about that and I shall write to him.

The memorandum of understanding provides for capital gains tax to be paid on gains from the disposal of private assets and on the private proportion of capital gains on the assets of the privy purse. Assets of the Duchies of Lancaster and Cornwall do not belong to the Queen or the Prince of Wales and are not theirs to dispose of. The duchies may sell assets from time to time, but the policy is to apply any proceeds to maintain their capital base for the future. Capital gains are not distributed and, under the terms of the memorandum, there is no capital gains tax in such circumstances. The position is not dissimilar to rollover relief that exists within the system.

As for inheritance tax, the memorandum of understanding recognises the need for assets to pass to successive sovereigns if the monarchy, as an institution, is to continue to play its part in the nation's affairs and to have some financial independence. It therefore provides for assets to pass from one sovereign to another without the payment of inheritance tax, but if the sovereign makes gifts or bequests to another person other than the new sovereign, the normal inheritance tax rules operate as they do for all members of the community. There are no special rules for other members of the royal family. They are fully liable to tax on the same basis as the rest of us.

The hon. Gentleman kindly drew attention to fact that the civil list annual report has been published for the first time. It now joins the annual reports on grant in aid for the maintenance of occupied royal palaces and grant in aid for royal air and train travel. Such documents are available for scrutiny. The audit position was endorsed by Ministers as recently as 1998 after consultation with the then leader of Her Majesty's Opposition. That reflects the clear and long-standing bipartisan policy that accounts should not be laid before Parliament, or be subject to national audit scrutiny. However, the accounts are audited in accordance with the high standards of all auditing – and how the money is spent is also thoroughly explained.

The hon. Gentleman asked whether the memorandum had been varied in any way in recent years. It might amuse him to learn that minor changes have been made to take account of the introduction of the self-assessment system. Those are the only changes. That reinforces the point that – except in the unique circumstances of transfer from sovereign to sovereign – the usual tax system operates.

The hon. Gentleman also asked about gifts received. He has not yet been given responses to a parliamentary question that he asked about that, and to a parliamentary question on a different matter, and I apologise to him for that. We have not yet received all of the information that he asked for, and we are checking what we have received, but his question will be answered. Gifts received in an official capacity belong to the nation; if Her Majesty receives a gift when she is performing her official role, that belongs to the nation. However, gifts received in a personal capacity are subject to the usual tax rules.

The hon. Gentleman asked about the art collection and, for instance, the use that is made of the revenue from entry fees into the palaces. I have forgotten the name of the charitable trust that was mentioned. I hope that the hon. Gentleman will forgive me for that, but I shall write to him about it. There are other relevant issues, such as the exact terms of the holding of the works of art on behalf of the nation, the obligation to maintain them, and the use of those monies to contribute to that.

The hon. Gentleman also asked about the surplus in the civil list. He may well have views about whether the agreement of 10 years ago should have been struck, but it was, and it must be honoured. A surplus has arisen, and I understand that it is being used to pay for maintenance of the palaces and public buildings. I believe that the contribution is about £7.5 million, and that the rest is drawn down from the surplus. However, I shall double check all of that to ensure that he receives accurate information.

I come now to the matter of the civil list and annuities. The Queen repays directly to the Treasury – and back into the Consolidated Fund – the annuities for all the members of the Royal family, other than those paid to the Duke of Edinburgh in relation to his official duties.

Therefore, the hon. Gentleman can see that in all respects – with the exception of the exclusion of inheritance tax due to the unique circumstances of transfer from sovereign to sovereign – the usual rules of the tax system that would be applicable to the rest of us are followed. The provisions with regard to transfer from sovereign to sovereign are a recognition of the role of the monarchy, and they seek to maintain its independence from the Government of the day.

As time is short, I undertake to double check the accuracy of my answers to the hon. Gentleman's questions and, if there are any questions that I have not answered in this brief response, I shall ensure that he receives that information. I am grateful to him for the way that he has pursued this morning's debate, and the straightforward and supportive fashion in which he has genuinely sought information on an area that is of interest to all our citizens who have celebrated the great contribution that Her Majesty the Queen has made to our nation with her family in this jubilee year.

Hansard Extract No. 3
House of Lords 15 July 2002
Genetically Modified Organisms

Lord Taverne: My Lords, whether one agrees or disagrees with Prince Charles's speech about genetically engineered crops or with his denunciation of cheap food, we must all agree that, in a constitutional monarchy, it is quite wrong for the heir to the throne to make speeches about politically controversial issues. If he wishes to do so, should he not renounce his claim to the throne?

The Lord Privy Seal (Lord Williams of Mostyn): My Lords, what is quite wrong is for any aspersions or reflection to be cast on the Sovereign or any member of the Royal Family. I would advise your Lordships not to accept such questions.

Hansard Extract No. 4
House of Lords 27 March 2003
The Monarchy

Lord Dormand of Easington asked Her Majesty's Government: Whether they will recommend the establishment of a Select Committee to consider the future of the Monarchy.

The Lord Privy Seal (Lord Williams of Mostyn): My Lords, no.

Lord Dormand of Easington: My Lords, is my noble and learned friend aware of the decreasing support for the monarchy, caused largely because people are against an unelected head of state? For that and other reasons, is it not time for a wide-ranging examination of the status of the monarchy, which could be undertaken by a Select Committee?

Lord Williams of Mostyn: My Lords, I do not believe that there is decreasing support for the monarchy. Recent history – the Jubilee year – demonstrates that. So, when my noble friend Lord Dormand asks me again for my answer, it is 'No'.

Lord Strathclyde: My Lords, notwithstanding the views of those who share the opinion of the noble Lord, Lord Dormand of Easington, is the noble and learned Lord aware that most people in this country will be immensely encouraged by what the Leader of the House has said? On behalf of Her Majesty's loyal Opposition we concur entirely.

Lord Williams of Mostyn: My Lords, yes.

Lord Smith of Clifton: My Lords, does the noble and learned Lord the Leader of the House agree with me that one does not have to be a republican to believe that it would be in the interests of the monarchy for a review to be held now in the light of its role in modern circumstances, particularly with regard to the exercise of the Royal prerogative?

Lord Williams of Mostyn: My Lords, I am aware of the current political – and perhaps legal – debate about the Royal prerogative. I know that views on the matter are strongly held, not always by republicans, as the noble Lord says. But this is a specific Question, with which I think I have dealt to the general satisfaction of noble Lords.

Lord Blaker: My Lords, will the noble and learned Lord suggest to his noble friend Lord Dormand that he might get together with me to make a survey of the states around the world that have elected heads of state – there are perhaps 150 – to see whether he wishes to reconsider his views?

Lord Williams of Mostyn: My Lords, yes.

Lord Carter: My Lords, we have heard the views of the Official Opposition. Is my noble and learned friend aware of the views of the Liberal Democrats?

Lord Williams of Mostyn: My Lords, they do not normally have any.

Lord Roper: My Lords, I thought that the Government had noticed that we have them at least in the Division Lobby from time to time. But we appreciate the Lord Privy Seal's reply to the Question.